Prof.Karen Lacey

How To Be A Good Brother

This book was professionally typeset on Reedsy

Find out more at reedsy.com

Contents

    1.

    2.

    3.

    4.

1

INTRODUCTION

Sibling relationships are regarded as extremely important. The majority of people believe that it is a wonderful feeling to have an older or younger brother. Siblings have a special bond that is based on love and respect for one another.

A good sibling supports their siblings in achieving their goals and interests. They are one of their top team promoters, and the group would cheer them on loudly. Additionally, because they are pleased with their achievements, they celebrate with their siblings. Additionally, they assist them in achieving their goals.

2

What Make a Good Portrait Of a Brother

A brother is more than just another family member. It is possible for siblings to influence one another's lives, act as positive role models, and offer one another assistance when needed. A good brother can influence the social and emotional growth of a younger sibling and serve as a role model for how to act in school and with friends. One of the best ways a brother can influence his siblings is by modeling positive behavior for them. Younger siblings can benefit from a positive role model by being able to better navigate social decisions, perform better academically and professionally, and be better able to make good decisions about their family or relationships. A positive older brother can have an impact on his younger sibling's academic performance, according to studies. Older siblings who reported high levels of academic engagement had a positive impact on younger siblings.

While friends can change over time, a good brother stays with someone for a long time. Family members have a unique and special bond with one another, in contrast to friendships, which typically include a deeper understanding of one another. Years of living together yield this deeper knowledge in addition to the shared history. While a brother may be able to provide the same level of companionship as a friend, he is less likely to move on to a new social setting than a friend. It has been shown that having a healthy relationship with one's older brother increases the likelihood that the younger sibling will have healthy feelings of self-worth and show fewer signs of depression as the child moves into middle childhood and adolescence.

Is Tactful While Being Honest

Honesty is an essential part of any healthy relationship. Family and siblings are especially important for this quality. A good brother ought to be open and honest with his siblings. Because of this, he shouldn't tell the brutal truth. If the truth is revealed without tact, a sibling may experience distress and feelings of hurt. For example, claiming that your brother's ex-girlfriend left him because he was unattractive and didn't look good in clothes is likely to cause conflict. On the other hand, if your brother wants to get women's attention, you should tell him he can change his clothes and offer to help. This demonstrates your sincerity without being mean.

Has a Good Ear

Not all brothers are able to communicate effectively by instructing siblings. Before responding, a good brother actively listens to his siblings and processes what they have to say. Active listening is the practice of paying attention to what the other person is saying in order to comprehend their point of view.

Supportive of their siblings

A good sibling is one who is supportive of their siblings and encourages them to pursue their interests and goals. They are some of their best cheerleaders, and the audience would boo them on. Additionally, because they are pleased with their achievements, they celebrate with their siblings. They also help them achieve their goals and are always available for assistance. Siblings naturally want to care for one another because they are family members. Some would even go above and beyond in order to assist their siblings. Even if they have their own problems, they are unable to say no to their siblings who require assistance. Always considerate A good brother or sister never forgets the birthdays of their siblings. During Christmas and other special occasions, you can anticipate them giving you wonderful presents and hosting surprise parties for you. They will also be thrilled to attend their plays, graduations, and other important events.

A brother that can be counted on to be honest and trustworthy.

They promise to keep their sister or brother's shared information private. They are unlikely to betray their siblings, even in the event of misunderstandings.

defends their siblings

A brother or sister who is loyal to their siblings is one who defends them. Because they are so protective of them, they can even step in for their siblings when they need to. Together with their siblings, they will fight and defend them.

Another quality of a good sibling is being sincere and honest with them.

They tell their siblings the truth and are honest. When they are aware that their siblings need to hear the truth, they will be truthful. Because of this, they are adept at reprimanding.

corrects their mistakes regarding

When necessary, a good sibling corrects and reprimands their siblings. They won't allow wrongdoing to occur.

Offers advice based on their own experience

Siblings who care about their siblings, particularly the older ones, will give them advice that is useful and can be used right away. The majority of the time, they will typically derive their wisdom from their own personal experiences.

teaches them to respect their parents.

Brothers and sisters who are kind to one another are also kind to one another. One of the best things a good brother or sister can do for their other siblings is to respect their parents. They will teach them to honor and obey their parents even if they are imperfect.

Good leader

The younger members of the family can learn a lot from an excellent older sibling. They are good at making decisions and can enforce house rules with firmness. They also show their parents how to raise good children by taking initiative to do household chores. Naturally, they're also good at delegating work.

Generous and selfless

A selfless sibling is also an admirable sibling. When they have the money, they will spoil their siblings and buy them gifts. They can also put their desires aside to help their siblings with their responsibilities.

Does not compete with siblings

You can also say that a sibling is beneficial if they do not view their siblings as rivals. They have no desire for them. They consider their own success to be their siblings' success. In order to assist their siblings, some are even willing to give up their own goals.

Apologizes when wronged.

A good sibling is also humble. They can accept their mistakes and apologize for them. In addition, they are open to corrections.

initiates reconciliation

Additionally, when there is a miscommunication, the mature sibling will not only apologize for their mistakes. By putting their pride aside, they can also begin a process of reconciliation. They are so in love with their siblings that they won't let a day go by when they didn't disagree with one another.

forgives and doesn't hold grudges

A good brother or sister doesn't live in rage and resentment. They are able to forgive them and let go of their anger and pain because of their siblings.

provides time for siblings to bond.

Even if their siblings are busy with their own lives and careers, a wonderful sibling will always find time to spend time with them. In addition, they initiate family get-together, schedule them, and plan vacations for holidays.

takes care of them

You don't have to ask a good sibling for help when a brother or sister is sick. Because they have an unwavering love for their family, they will be willing to give up whatever they are doing to help a sibling who is in need.

Understanding and patience

A good brother or sister has a lot of patience and empathy for their sister or brother. Despite the fact that sometimes misunderstandings and arguments cannot be avoided, they will still do their best to tolerate their siblings' flaws.

As a matter of course, a responsible sibling is an excellent role model for the other siblings. This has a particularly negative impact on the older siblings. They will try to be good children, especially as students. They will study their lessons on a regular basis and strive for high grades. Some people even put off starting a love life while they are still in school to avoid being distracted.

prays for their siblings.

Another quality of a good sibling is their capacity for prayer. Out of love for their brothers and sisters, they beg God for their success, health, direction, and safety. They are aware that they cannot always be together, despite the fact that God will always be by their side. Because of this, they pray to the Lord that He will always protect them.

3

How To Love Your Siblings

How to Love Your Sisters and Brothers

Find out what they like to do.

You ought to assist them in any way possible.

Don't limit your gift-giving to special occasions.

Go out with them from time to time.

Conversations with them should be intimate.

Be a trustworthy secret keeper.

Listen to them.

Try not to irritate them too much.

Put past disputes behind you.

Give them an apology right away.

Be humble.

Keep an eye on them at all times.

Encourage them to accomplish their objectives.

Make it appear as though you are not a rival.

Don't be afraid to give them a hug.

4

What Is The Bible's Position Regarding Brothers

There are many different brothers mentioned in the Bible. Sadly, there were love-filled relationships and hate-filled relationships. Brothers by blood are not always mentioned in Scripture. Brotherhood can refer to close friendships.

can be other believers who are a part of the body of Christ. It might even be additional soldiers. Most of the time, brothers have strong bonds.

As Christians, we are to support our brothers. We are not supposed to hurt them; rather, we should always help our brothers succeed.

We are expected to love, assist, and make amends for our siblings. Thank God for your brother. No matter if your brother is a Christian coworker, friend, brother, or sibling, you should always keep them in your prayers.

Invoke God to shape them, guide them, and improve their love for one another. Always treat brothers with respect because they are always a part of the same family.

In Christianity, brothers and sisters are as close as hands and feet.

There is no need for brothers to talk to each other; They can simply sit together in a room and feel at ease immediately.

The prayer meeting fulfills the spiritual brotherhood's request due to its greater exclusivity and direct fitness than any other religious worship ordinance. People who share similar values can confer and enter into a covenant with one another to jointly make a unique promise to God. The prayer meeting is a unique way to cultivate Christian graces and to encourage personal and social growth. It is a divine command that is rooted in the social nature of man.

"Let brotherly love continue,says Hebrews 13:1.

According to Romans 12:10, be brotherly in your devotion to one another. honorably prioritize one another.

Last but not least, you all need to live in harmony, be sympathetic, love one another as if they were brothers, and be humble and kind to one another.

It is expected of us to take care of our brother.

The LORD asked Cain, "Where is your brother Abel?in Genesis 4:9. He said, I don't know in response: Am I concerned about my brother?

Hatred of your brother Leviticus 19:17 You are not required to have a strong dislike for your brother. You must immediately correct your fellow citizen to avoid sinning against him.

As stated in 1 John 3:15, you are aware that no one who commits murder has eternal life.

Brotherly relationships are adored by God.

Psalm 133:1: See how pleasant and beneficial living with brothers is!

You always have true brothers by your side.

"A brother is born for a difficult time, and a friend loves at all times," says Proverbs 17:17.

According to Proverbs 18:24, a man with many friends can still be destroyed, but a true friend stays closer than a brother.

Jesus Christ's Brothers, Matthew 12:46–50: While Jesus was speaking to the crowd, his mother and brothers stood outside and asked to speak with him. Someone informed Jesus that his brothers and mother were outside and wanted to talk to him. He was asked about his mother by Jesus. After that, he declared, "Look, these are my brothers and mother." After that, he pointed to his followers. Those who do my Heavenly Father's will are my mother, sister, and brother!

He refers to those who are made holy as brothers and sisters because they come from the same place, according to Hebrews 2:11–12.

A brother is always there to help.

2 Corinthians 11:9 Also, when I needed something while I was with you, the brothers from Macedonia provided it, so I wasn't a burden to anyone. I will continue to avoid causing you unnecessary stress by doing so.

"How can God's love dwell in anyone who has this world's goods and sees his brother in need but closes his eyes to his need?" is the question posed in 1 John 3:17–18. Little ones, we must love with truth and action, not words and speech.

In James 2:15–17, take a brother or sister who does not have access to food and clothing on a daily basis. Keep them warm and fed, but don't forget to take care of their physical needs if anyone says, "Go in peace." In a similar vein, faith on its own is meaningless if it is not accompanied by action.

40 of Matthew 25: "I tell you the truth, you did it for me, just as you did it for one of the least of these brothers or sisters of mine," the king will respond.

Brothers deserve our deepest affection.

As Jonathan and David did, we are to show agape love.

2 Samuel 1:26 Oh, Jonathan, my brother, how I grieve for you! Oh, how much I loved you! Furthermore, your devotion to me was greater than any devotion to a woman (John 3:16). We learned about love this way: He gave His life for our sake. We ought to also sacrifice our lives for our brothers.

1 Samuel 18:1 Upon Jonathan's completion of his conversation with Saul, he came to the realization that David's soul was intertwined with his own and that Jonathan loved David as if he were his own soul.

Brotherhood in the Bible: Genesis 33:4 Esau dashed to Jacob's side. Esau wrapped him around him, kissed him, and embraced him. They both wept.

Genesis 45:14–15 He then wept and embraced Benjamin as he wrapped his arms around him. He wept over his brothers as well, kissing them on the cheek. After that, he had a conversation with his brothers.

4:18 of Matthew While Jesus was strolling alongside the Sea of Galilee, he came upon Simon, whom he referred to as Peter, and Andrew, two brothers. They were inserting a net into the lake because they were fishermen.

Genesis 25:24–26 states, Behold, when her labor and delivery days were over, she had twins in her womb." Because the first one was red and had hair covering his entire body, they named him Esau.

When his brother emerged from the cave carrying Esau's heel, he was given the name Jacob. Isaac was 60 when she gave birth to them.

5

A Good Son

Having a son is one of life's most rewarding experiences. A child must be a good son in order to be a good brother. However, the lack of clear guidelines for raising morally upright children makes it an adventure as well.

You can instill these important traits in your children as you raise them to be successful adults. A good son has a lot of important qualities.

The children we raise will become the role models we set for these young people. Children learn from their parents, no matter how good or bad they are.

How can a child be a good son

Having a son is a wonderful blessing when it comes to raising the next generation of men. Particularly in this world, it is essential to raise strong, protective men who are not afraid to express their feelings.

You can offer a child a few pieces of advice that will assist him in becoming a good son.

Maintain open communication with your parents, regardless of how close you are to them. It is essential to keep them informed. Clearly communicate to them what you hold most dear.

In your conversations, be candid about your hopes and fears. Remember that they've been through it.

A son ought to be able to discuss anything he wants with his parents. It is absolutely necessary for the son's parents to speak up.

Parents want their children to be as happy as possible and to have lives that are meaningful and full of meaning.

Parents will gladly assist their children if they are aware of their children's requirements and have the resources to meet them. To accomplish this successfully, it is essential for parents and children to communicate openly with one another.

Parents must also communicate with their children about their plans, feelings, and actions. This gives children the impression that they are a part of the family and can influence its future.

Children must be heard by their parents and given the freedom to make their own decisions. If parents talk to their children about their interests, aspirations for the future, friends, and so on, Learn to make well-informed decisions for yourself to become a self-reliant man. The relationship will be bolstered and made more open as a result of this.

It's okay to rely on others for some things, but you have to make your own decisions about your life.

Despite how much it hurts to think about it, keep in mind that your parents won't be around forever.

We should treasure our time with our parents before they pass away, according to an old saying. We shouldn't wait for them to get sick or die before we appreciate them and spend time with them because life is unpredictable.

Spending time with loved ones, both young and old, is essential.

If you are confident that they will value your time with them, the effort will be well worth it. Taking the time to encourage children to value their individual time with their parents is also worthwhile.

Due to the abundance of distractions in today's society, it can be challenging to disconnect from technology and spend quality time with loved ones or friends. However, it is essential to prioritize time spent with others because everyone occasionally has busy schedules.

In the grand scheme of things, life is short and precious. Spend as much time as possible with your parents. They will be more appreciative of your quality time with them than you are.

A quality that is frequently overlooked is gratitude. It's important to be grateful for the little things that happen in life. Doing this can help you feel better and help you develop a more positive outlook, even when things aren't going your way.

Your relationships with other people will also benefit from your gratitude.

While there are a variety of methods for expressing gratitude, thank-you notes are an easy one. When someone has helped us out, we should always make it a point to express our gratitude as soon as possible.

For private gratitude practice, you can also try writing in a gratitude journal or making gratitude a daily habit as part of your evening routine.

It's easy to forget how much you rely on and spend time with your parents. You must acknowledge everything they have done for you because they have put in a lot of effort to raise a good son.

Respect Your Parents These people gave you your life. If you treat them with the respect they deserve, they will treat you with respect. As a result, you will both gain a profound appreciation for one another.

Be devoted and trustworthy, especially to friends and family. Be true to your word and stand by the people you care about most.

The loyalty of a son is crucial because it has the potential to provide support and security in the future.

Loyalty is a character trait that can be applied to all aspects of life, regardless of the people you are interacting with.

Be helpful One of a son's most important qualities is being reliable.

One way to show that you can be counted on is to help out when you need to. Even if you lack the resources or expertise, you can still make a difference in someone's life by putting in a little time and effort.

Younger boys can develop a dependable work ethic with the help of a chore chart. Help other people, especially your parents, without hesitation. You want to show your parents that you can rely on them just like you did when you were a child.

Maintain a sense of humor and smile frequently.

Laughter is so essential to life that it can often save a person's life. It will help you deal with stress on a daily basis.

As you reminisce about happy times spent together, laugh with your loved ones.

Always be respectful of others, especially your parents and elders. Your manners will always stand out and be noticed.

Sons must learn manners from their parents. Be a good person and a person that people want to hang out with. When you meet someone for the first time, shake their hand or kindly greet them. Cover your mouth and ask for their pardon whenever they cough or sneeze. When someone does something nice for you, say please and thank you.Being delicate and kind conveys a gigantic measure of solidarity.

Always treat others with kindness.

Raising a boy is more than just teaching him to be tough or strong There's so much more to it than that. These characteristics of a good son need to be nurtured by all parents.

Printed in Great Britain
by Amazon

27987313R00020